S'FUNNY HOW YOU NEVER LAUGH AT THE TIME THOUGH, INNIT?

John Wright

Published by John Wright
Publishing partner: Paragon Publishing, Rothersthorpe
First published 2013
© John Wright 2013

ISBN 978-1-78222-107-4

Book design, layout and production management by Into Print
www.intoprint.net
01604 832149

Printed and bound in UK and USA by Lightning Source

2

CONTENTS

FOREWORD

1: EARLY DAYS	5
2: MARRIAGE	11
3: MY FATHER	13
4: PRISON	15
5: FREEDOM	17
6: THE FIGHTS	19
7: SECOND TIME AROUND	21
8: WOMEN	24
9: THE HOLOCAUST	26
10: DERBY ROYAL INFIRMARY	28
11: A DEDICATION	31
12: GOING HOME	33
13: NEW FREEDOM	35
14: HEADWAY	38
15: FROM THERAPY TO A DREAM	41
POSTSCRIPT	43

For Lindsay

FOREWORD

This book was written as therapy for me. I hope it may give help to others.

It's very much a 'street level' story but it's my life – I guess I've written as I speak as I've lived – anyway I haven't seen the other side.

I know it ain't all it should be but there again neither am I!

I remember how I used to look, most things in my life good or bad until the clock stopped on November 18th 1978 . . .

1 Early Days

I vaguely remember my family's first home. The chickens in the back garden, a nine inch TV, one of the first on our estate. We used to have a houseful of kids come to watch Superman or Lassie. Looking back to us kids this was Superman. I've seen it played back just recently and he wore a pair of baggy long johns with creases round the knees! The TV was as big as a sideboard with folding doors yet we had a magnifying glass positioned in front of it to see the nine inch screen.

I remember three ducks flying across the living room wall and we had massive leatherette chairs and a settee. Were they only 'Fee fi fo fum' size because we were little snotty nosed kids?

I can recall my Dad coming home from work black as soot with white circles around his eyes and mouth, pit helmet on and knee pads with a tin lunch box (no Tupperware in those days) possibly with a sooty old sandwich left in it and us kids wanting to eat it. The very early days having his tin bath filled and one of us scrubbing his back, D.H. Lawrence stuff but nice memories. His dinner on a saucepan of boiling water to keep hot but dried up and waiting for him to leave a spud or a bit of meat on his chop.

It's possible I wanted his leftovers because it was 'a man's dinner' and to eat what was left by a man was being 'a man' although I was only eight or nine years old.

I can still see my Dad coming down our street and me feeling quite proud he was a miner. In my eyes it made him a lot stronger and tougher than other kids' dads.

Our family was Dad (Bod), Mam and five children – Babs, Jim, me, Pauline and Stephen. We used to have happy times as a family and we were considered quite wealthy because Dad's income was far more than the average worker's. Shit he probably got £10 a week compared with the £6 of the others but we had a family car, a Morris 8 and went to the seaside every year. We were never rich because our parents lived up to the wages coming into our home but with Mam working scrubbing and cleaning we were rich in many ways going on holiday every year when most other families stayed on the estate. On the hols Pauline, Stephen and me were all dressed the same – baseball boots, black jeans with 'plant pot' turn ups and a knitted brown sweater, the cardigan type that Mam had knitted in between all her domestic chores. As kids we couldn't see any unhappiness in our parents only the odd skirmish that was over before it started.

The first school I went to was Southfields Infants and I wore an apron with an embroidered ship on it. We used to have a spoonful of olive oil (ugh!) followed by a spoonful of pure orange juice (hurray) and after playing outside we were then put down on camp beds for an hour in the afternoon. I always seemed to have an underpant leg showing out of my short trousers probably because they were my big brother's old ones handed down to 'get the wear out of them'. When the 'laggy' had gone you got both legs hanging out!

We moved to a new council estate. Everywhere seemed so fresh and green and most families tried to outdo the others. Every household drank from Coronation mugs and had wirelesses as big as tables. I went to a new school and played for their first football and cricket teams. We lost every match that first year but I met my first real friend there and our friendship was to rekindle at secondary school.

My first encounter with him was when playing cricket against my 'old' school from the 'rough' estate we had just left – we were better than them now eh? Every time our batsmen attempted a stroke we missed and some kid led an appeal with six or seven others and we were told be our teacher that only the bowler or wicket keeper were allowed to appeal. We all had to wear white and all these 'scruffs' were in jeans! Well if this 'scruff' wasn't bowling he would be in the slips appealing, his bowling terrified us and I think we were all out for five and three of those were byes. That was my first encounter with Vic. S'funny, even then he seemed to have the face of a much older person. Us kids were kids but he seemed about twenty-five and even the I used to call him Sid James because he looked so like the actor from the 'Carry On' films.

After Montrose my posh new Junior school I went to Linwood Boys secondary. It was quite different there, mainly boys from the old estate and I lose junior school pals because they mostly went to grammar school. I started the first term in the 'A' class and lasted two years at the top until, in the 3rd year, I was relegated to 3B the 'boys' class. Instead of feeling a failure I was overjoyed. Now, after two years of wearing a uniform and carrying a big satchel I became a mini 'Ted' wearing jeans and a big bouffant wave held in place by my sister's hair lacquer. My route to school changed and I went the longer way round to pass the girls' school. In my homemade 'drainys' and winkle picker shoes I would get wolf whistles which made me feel like Jack the Lad!

So, after a poor education which was my fault I suppose I started my first job as a hosiery trimmer. It lasted about four years working in a big factory with other kids my age partnering men and listening to the radio whistling or singing along with the music that was played. The stations were not much to the young men's liking but it was varied and we all sang along to 'I wanna hold your hand'. The old 'scrote' I worked with really pissed me off 'cos I ended up doing more than half the work but only got a third of the money!

One incident from my teenage years I remember was outside a Saturday night dance hall. I had just left for a moment but I had a pass out to go back in. There were a few people outside trying to get in but it was full. Anyway as I was knocking on the door this copper arrived to move the crowd on.

'But I have a pass out.'

'Now then lad, move on.'

'But these people want to go in for the first time and it's full but I have a pass out, I've been inside once can't you see?'

'Come on move it.'

'Wait, here's the doorman, he'll remember.'

It went on like this for a while until 'For the last time move . . . right you're nicked.'

So for a harmless trivial offence I was arrested. My first offence, a stained character I was stunned protesting my innocence and because

I was underage I was taken home and my Mam and Dad were told the story. They actually believed I was the leader of a gang outside the hall refusing to move. I expected their support, somebody had to believe me but not even Mam and Dad did.

This was a turning point towards the anti 'blue serge'.

Now I was paying my board and spending bits on clothes and drink never having any concern for tomorrow. Fact is I couldn't imagine being twenty one, it was so far away and so old! My friend was a lad who I nicknamed 'The Renna' (renegade). He was about 3 years older than me and a real eye-catcher for the girls. His clothes were really modern and his hair very long – in those days if your hair went over your ears you were a 'scruffy bastard'! Men were still going to the barber's and having a short back and sides with plenty off the top so this meant when they 'clipped' their fag and put it behind their ear you could see it.

The Renna's clothes were really way out and we went around town quite a lot together. He was a great dancer and fascinated me because I was a real wallflower when it came to dancing but he could jive!

We were seen escorting all the top girls in town. In the Palais we were treated with jealousy by a bunch of 'Townies' because we were not 'City Boys' yet we were pulling all the city girls. We wore fashionable Italian suits and Cuban heeled shoes and as The Renna has a Lambretta scooter we had a great time.

Suddenly this quiet boy from the Monsell estate was starting to get noticed in town and although we were never violent we seemed to be earmarked for violence because of our flash clothes.

One Saturday our football match was cancelled because of frost and a team-mate and I went to watch a team from a lower division whose pitch was not affected. Each team was a man short so we were asked to play on opposite sides. I scored four goals and so did he in a game drawn 8-8. We were quite a revelation!

In the team I played with were two brothers who really made a fuss of us. I went down town the next day to the Palais and saw this townie from the football. He didn't have the best of looks and when I got to know him I used to piss take 'Nice to see you to see you nice' because of his Bruce Forsyth chin! He was always laughing, a dancer, fighter and a joker. His humour was infectious, I liked him instantly and he could pull the birds so we chatted and arranged to meet up again. This was the start of Johnny Wright and the Townie era - an era of fighting and picking up girls . . .

I'd had a few fights when I was young but only "My Dad can fight your Dad" fights so seeing this young townie perform amazed me. He was a cheat using anything within reach to win but I admired him immensely. The violence of today was created by my generation – kicking, glassing, nutting, gouging. The townie wouldn't argue. 'If you're angry, fight' was his answer. What was the point in delaying the inevitable? This is how I felt during this period of my life. I couldn't wait to see him again and although I've never had homosexual tendencies I loved this boy and was always excited about seeing him. He would pull a few strokes from time to time but he would be there in your corner if you needed him.

I remember one incident from this time that still makes me smile. At the barber's were pictures of idols from the era all over his walls so I chose one style thinking I'd look like the star I'd chosen then wallop! The barber began to savage my head, he went berserk and I knew immediately I had made a terrible mistake. I was halfway out of the chair wanting to get away but he was conducting a symphony on my 'barnet' like a comic dentist one leg on the floor the other on my chair. He was still cutting my hair as I was putting my coat on – "I've just got to level it up lad".

'S'alright, s'alright!' I eventually got out of the shop looking like a cross between Henry IV and Gilbert O'Sullivan. I raced home to salvage what was left of it but it was useless and Friday night was music night as well.

Anyway I got myself dressed up trying to look half decent but it was no use, I looked a right mess. I met up with all my friends on our estate and went into town but it was ridicule every few seconds. All night this went on 'What the hell's happened to you?' Going home around 2.0am I passed the barber's shop and with ridicule still ringing in my ears I picked up a brick and threw it through the shop window.

The next day in the local pub there was the barber playing 'Dommies' so I popped over to hear what they were talking about. He lives above his shop and was telling his mates how he was looted last night. "Ciggies, money. combs. Brylcream, condoms – the bastards cleared my shop out."

He was obviously doing an insurance claim and had nipped downstairs to do 'the looting' himself.

I was even more topped – he was going to make money out of my anger! I couldn't say anything though so just stood there bursting to point to my head and yell "This is why your window went in!"

AGED 17, LIVING IN EYRES MONSELL

2 MARRIAGE

My girlfriend was called Sue. We were ready to be married in church but I had second thoughts. At twenty I was far too young so I called it off and ended our relationship. Then she paid my Mam and Dad a visit and told them she was pregnant and in those days (1965) your parents made sure you got married. There was hardly any 'living together' or abortions or single parents. They insisted I got married – "You've made your bed lad" but I dug my heels in and argued and argued refusing to get married.

My brother visited and told me not to be stupid. He and his wife had their ups and downs but they were happy and he thought I should 'Do the right thing'.

To get out of the flak I agreed to marry her thinking F.C.Dobbsie style (a character in the film Sierra Madre who ends up talking to himself) that once I was married I'd leave but for now I'd do anything to shut them up. I never once thought about the severity of the situation and how it would destroy lives. A few months after the wedding my brother and his wife split up and were divorced.

We lived with my sister whose husband was away in the navy and I began to think about what had happened to my life. I was so restless and didn't know which way to turn so I cleared off to Margate.

We all went down there on scooters, a whole gang of us. I had never seen anything like it before – gang warfare, punch ups, deck chairs floating out to sea and rockers thrown off the pier. We ran off as the Police moved in and ducked into a side street just watching and about two hundred 'Mods' followed us. It was unbelievable – shops and cafes wrecked, cars stopped in the road windows smashed total chaos.

A mate had a Daily Mail rolled up in his hand and was arrested for carrying an offensive weapon but that was the confusion it brought about. Anyone dressed as a mod running in the streets was arrested and I suppose we were part of the pack but only running to get away from the rest however once you're in front they follow like a herd of antelopes. It was a bit comical really in front shouting 'Don't follow us' but still they kept coming!

For a while home was forgotten but it had to be faced so I went back to my wife. She was now nearing the birth so we got a flat of our own, a bit of a dump but it would have to do.

When the birth was starting I dashed off to call an ambulance and when it came and we climbed inside she started screaming that the baby was coming. I asked the driver to go faster but the man sitting in the back with us said he'd been on hundreds of calls like these and . . . 'Sod me Jack hurry up it's coming' . . . and a little head appeared!

My daughter was born. It was earth shattering.

MARGATE MOD

3 MY FATHER

For some time my parents' relationship had been breaking down and things got even worse. Mam left home and only my sister knew where she'd gone yet would not say and I will never forgive her for that 'cos poor old Bod was really tormented. He lost weight, became pathetic and was a totally different man. He just got worse and all he wanted to do was confront her and her new boyfriend face to face but it wasn't to be.

Should I have done more? Should others have done more?

'My Mam gone away with another bloke, no Dad you've got that wrong. What for, she's our Mam, what are we going to do?' What's Dad going to do, hold on you will heal please Dad don't go under.

I got up, made the tea then lit the fire. That's funny, Dad had not lit the fire. At the back of my brain I feel something's wrong but I dare not discover the truth. Well it's quite late now so I must go and wake Dad but I know don't I? He's dead. I've been too scared to find out but it still has to be faced.

'Dad, Dad do you want a cup of tea?' as I knock on his bedroom door. Silence, I must go in, go on John go in. The first thing I see is a note propped up and addressed to me. I do not see my Dad just that bloody note. Look at your Dad you fool, it could be a mistake but no, he's dead the poor man.

I was completely shattered and it's continued to mess up my brain since.

We stayed on at Dad's house and we all tried to readjust then on the day of the funeral I was already putting square pegs into round holes and ready to start basket weaving when my mother hit me with a volley.

"I'm going to tell him." Everyone who knew what she meant started to hold her back and threaten her.

"Don't, you do and I'll kill you," shouted my brother.

"Go on, tell me what?" I'm acting the big shot.

"I don't know why you're so upset, he wasn't even your Dad."

I couldn't act tough about that. 'What did she say' I kept repeating even though I'd heard very clearly. My mouth kept gulping and I didn't want people to see the effect her words had on me but I didn't need a psychoanalyst to tell me what was wrong. Something had been instilled in me that was to change my life. It was HATE. I was a 'brimmer' with it. If I could have directed it, channelled it into boxing perhaps I could have been a force to be reckoned with but sadly that hate began to destroy my life and those who shared it with me. The family I knew had been destroyed overnight and this was the beginning of me becoming a real bad ass.

I've not had much contact with my Mother since then. I feel she is indirectly responsible for what was to come – hatred, depression and violence creating pressure on my brain.

4 PRISON

Sue, my daughter and I went to live in a new maisonette. It was very modern but in a concrete jungle and families were carted off like cattle to live in them.

My friend, the Townie had married at the same time as us and lived opposite in a ground floor flat. We were on the second floor looking into his lounge and whenever one of us felt like having a drink we would signal with the arm motion of drinking and put up seven fingers to indicate 'I'll be round at 7.00.' The one waiting for the knock would sound so surprised. 'I wonder who that is? I really don't want to go out but he's called for me so I'll just have a couple. See you.' Then off we would go laughing and punching holes in the sky not caring what the morning would bring. For a few hours the young paternal problems were suppressed.

Shortly after we moved I had a scooter accident and suffered broken ribs. I was on the back of a mate's scooter and we were driving along quite carefully when this car passed sounding the horn and one of the passengers was on our football team. He was waving then the car cut in making us swerve and I went flying.

The car driver was taken to court and my solicitor had predicted I would get a few thousand if he was found guilty. Before the trial I told the bloke to just speak the truth and I'd give him £200 but for some reason he lied as they all do. I caught him out one night after he'd been in hiding for some weeks and he went pale. I set about him but he wouldn't fight. 'Come on yer bastard fight' but still no retaliation. When I left I was feeling really topped kicking bits of rubbish down the street in frustration!

We went for a holiday to Spain on the £200 out of court settlement money and one night my wife went to bed one night around midnight. I sat at the bar and the courier came to talk to me. She asked me to go to her room and I could have said I'm married but I didn't feel any loyalty to my wife. I didn't feel married, unfair of me I know but the 'Dobbsie' in me said you have to be in love to be married and as you're not in love it's ok.

When we went back home I was still being 'a bad ass' and in trouble with the law again. Me and a mate made plans to work on a building site on Jersey. I got a job as a labourer which was very boring but I earned good money and it was tax free. I thought I would be able to sort out my domestic aches on this island but the next day my mate announced he was going home. Back he went to his love nest . . .

'I didn't want to go love, it was Wrighty's idea I only wanted a holiday' and she believed him.

When I arrived back a couple of weeks later I was fighting again and got picked up by the police. This time I was taken to court and received a prison sentence.

Prison just destroyed me. It's a deterrent if you value your freedom and going to the toilet without someone checking if your feet and head are visible! So as not to think of sex I read so many cowboy books I used to begin letters to my wife with "Dear Sioux", it really messed me up.

I knew this kid working in the kitchen and on my second say he told me never to eat the porridge. 'Why, why' I asked. Then he told me the cons who worked there used to w... well I can't tell you what they used to do to the porridge but it was pretty disgusting. 'But I've already had some!'

The stench of that place was awful. I only served a six month sentence and I think subconsciously I wanted to go there to get my life straightened out. I've always kept the fear of going back so I guess I learned something from my visit if only NOT TO EAT PORRIDGE!

1968 - 23 YEARS OLD

5 Freedom

Isoon drifted back to my old kind of life on release but I did try my hardest most times to keep out of trouble. I was never a thief just sometimes my temper would get so bad I was like a kettle only I didn't have an automatic switch off. I didn't know about any of these symptoms building up, vessels stretching and stretching in my brain, high blood pressure, violent headaches – I just put everything down to booze.

I was a big shot in terms of fighting and was put on a pedestal so although I thought I was very wise and clever I was nothing. It hurts to discover this but I wasn't very bright at all. Thinking I was somebody when I was around the pubs and clubs in the city really gave me this false image. I would act out a charade every time I was out then when it came to being me I would tear myself apart. When I was sober nobody really got to know me at all. People can claim to know me and give their version of what sort of person I was but it was only the part of me I gave them. If it had been filmed I would have won an Oscar!

That was possibly one of the reasons for increasing pressure on my brain – never allowing myself to be myself and always playing to the crowd. If the company I was in talked intelligently about politics then the old chameleon would adapt get on his soapbox and debate. Then if other people talked of who they'd laid or wanted to lay I would join in with that too, after all with my negative outlook on life womanising was my specialist subject.

Always I would have to act then if I heard how I was being described it would hurt because I knew it wasn't me, that is where the act fell apart. Instead of being satisfied that I had fooled so many it would hurt because they were wrong about me.

The pressure on my brain from my dad's suicide then being told he wasn't my father plus this continuous deception kept building up. It is good that I can look back over my life and pinpoint where events affected me. Other people can give their version but my version is what I have to live with so I'll accept only that.

Although my wife allowed me to move back in I was still bad news. Every Tuesday and Thursday night I would pay our neighbour Mrs S from the corner flat a visit. I was supposed to have gone football training but I would walk by her entry do a quick 'double take' for the coast to be clear then do my training on her! I would come home more wrecked than if I'd trained. I'd have to wet my kit so everything seemed in order. Wet kit, me knackered wife saying 'If it's that hard don't go next week!'

Later my wife told me that Mrs S was pregnant – 'I wonder who's been paying her visits 'cos her husband left ages ago. I've not seen her with anyone, have you John?'

Some time after that I heard a knock at the door and when I opened it there was Mrs S looking 'swell'. I slammed the door in her face but then the wife's in the hallway wondering what was going on. She opened the door and saw Mrs S.

'What do you want?' I'm in the hallway biting my nails and running on the spot like Jack Duckworth in Coronation Street.

'I've come to tell you that this is his' pointing at her lump.

'You what' I said. 'You're just after someone to name so you can get your allowance off the state now your husband has left.'

There was a big argument between her and me with the wife coming in now and then to my defence. She left with all kinds of threats and the wife saying 'Yeah you do that.'

I thought she believed me but when the front door closed – 'Now then you dirty b......'

I tried my best to lie my way out of it but she was not thick. She knew.

ME IN MY 'MRS S' DAYS

18

6 The Fights

My wife and I were fighting. I guess we always were but once this was a bit more and she fled the house. On her return I wouldn't let her in so she went off threatening to fetch the police. 'Fetch the law, see if I'm bothered' was my shouting goodbye.

A while later I was in Levis, no shirt sock or shoes and there was a knock on the door and there were two baby-faced policemen with 'Waffen S.S.' peaked caps over their noses. They asked if my wife could be allowed back in the house. I said 'Yes' but angrily shut the door. I was about to bolt it when 'Wallop' the door was hanging off its hinges with one of the 'Waffen S.S.' legs following it. After he had steadied himself from his one-legged entry he began his questionnaire and all the time he was speaking he would be smacking one fist into the palm of his other hand then tugging at his glove. He really was 'on set' and enjoying himself. I was asking him about the damaged plaster and wood and why he didn't knock. He was egging me on to get angry but although inside I was, I kept calm.

John Wayne did something similar in 'Brannigan' when he kicked down the door and then stepped inside and said 'Knock, knock' but this was real and they wouldn't go.

Well, as in most domestic quarrels if there had been an older copper there it would probably have been sorted out quite peacefully. When a married couple are having a 'domestic' they don't need a third party to dictate to them 'cos in most cases they will both turn on the third one and be united again. In an explosive situation like this they should act 'Helen Keller', hearing and seeing nothing because just by being there it will soon be over but not with these two. Suddenly I was twisted around with my arms up my back being taken out of my home. I put one leg up to the door entry and stopped myself on the wall. Their grip tightened but they couldn't move me. I kicked off the wall and then I was fee. As I dashed for the landing of the flats and reached the door to the stairs the first copper was about to arrest me. 'For what? What the hell have I done?' My temper was really explosive now. 'Look, it's over now, let me go home and you can report back to the nick. No punches have been thrown, me and her are ok now so let's just forget the whole thing.'

But not these boys, they really wanted to beat the shit out of me. They rushed me but not together so I knocked the first 'Sparko' motionless on the landing quickly followed by the second.

'You won't half be in trouble' says the wife and I was in a right dilemma. I couldn't work it out or think straight and was running up and down like Oliver Norville Hardy with echoes of 'Oooh! do something to help me!' I ran off through the estate but really only circling myself as the sound of the police cordon was all around me.

I knocked on 'The Townie's' door and dashed straight through past him to his lounge window that gave me a view of my flat and the police operation. It was really ridiculous that in my panic I was laughing at the events but the laughing included fear. There was nothing I could do so I made my barefoot way to surrender.

When the police saw me they made a mad dash to get me each racing the other to get his 'pips' to be the first to make an arrest. Even then it was like a rugby pack arrest and I was bundled into their van to be taken to the station and charged.

First I went into a cell then three policemen came to give me their form of punishment for raising a hand to 'The Blue Serge.' I'm not stupid this time. I'm not going to fight back as they begin to throw right-handers to the body (never the face). I really went over the top with cries of pain 'no more please, no more' and after a while they left. I uncurled from my ball really quite pleased with my convincing act.

Then I was charged – more pressure on my brain and another unnecessary stain on my character!

7 Second Time Around

After a time I met a beautiful girl and fell instantly in love. Perhaps I wanted it to change the direction of my life. I didn't like the course I was on or even myself but with her helping me, redirecting me perhaps I could learn to live with myself again.

As well as being beautiful she had a bubbly personality and was full of confidence and very intelligent. If it had run its natural course the affair might have ended but her bourgeois parents found out about us after our first date. I had stupidly left her phone number in my jacket and my first wife had telephoned the girl's father who came to me and said 'If you love each other, leave your wife and I'll help you all I can.'

The feelings I had for this girl were so unreal to me, she had cleansed me and I loved her so much. I had done a lot of lusting, living together and talking about love at different times in my life but the big one is only once.

I went to live in a dirty bedsit to save money for a divorce and a house. Living there was so destructive for me, it was like being in a cell again only I wasn't three'd (three in a cell) and didn't have to slop out but then my bank balance began to rise and it wasn't so bad. I was finally accepted by her middle class parents and we saved and saved.

But something bad was happening to me that I couldn't see. They were doing their best to turn me into a nice 'middle class fellow' and were succeeding because I loved her and I wanted to improve and better myself for her. If only I could have kept my natural identity and beliefs then anything else she could have had. There were plenty of rough edges to chip away at but leave the real Johnny Wright alone. I let it happen though and I can't blame them entirely because I should have made a stand very early in our relationship.

My divorce was now final, I had suppressed the hate and I had a beautiful young woman helping me to resurrect my life. We were buying our home and finally the wedding day arrived. All went well and we set off on our honeymoon to London for the weekend, saw the premiere of 'The Sting' and had a really good time.

Back in out new home everything went sour so quickly. She wanted a baby. Not next year or when things had eased financially but now. I wanted to learn to drive, a stereo, clothes and a holiday abroad – all material I know but I was doing a job I hated so 'let me have some material things to hate it with.'

'You already have a daughter so that's why you don't want another baby.'

'I don't believe this, I gave her up for you.'

She finally worked on me to agree to her coming off the pill saying it could be years before she got pregnant but after a few weeks she was pregnant and my life did a complete circle again. Everything went sour, it was an impossible situation, the living, our relationship so I packed my cleanest dirty shirt and left home. Her father gave me £200 to go and there wouldn't be any maintenance if I signed the house over to her. I was heartbroken, I kept smacking my forehead with the palm of my hand 'Yes it's happening, beam me up Scotty.'

So once again there was this terrific pressure on my brain with no outlet. I was very near now almost November 1978. Wherever I went or whatever I did it was never far enough from my grief, anger and a broken heart so what do I do when the pressure is strong and I have the blues – drink. I was successful for a few hours but the bigger pain of violence was destroying not only me but those around who loved me. I had to hate people who loved me because that was a way of hurting myself, inflicting my own punishment.

Now I am able to look back into my life before November 1978 and get to the root of the problems. I wouldn't have listened before because I thought I was right no matter what course I took but I was so sick and on the edge I am only pleased I never killed anyone. That might sound dramatic but I was so close, bruises heal and they will say 'John who?' so that's ok.

No matter how much pain I inflicted I was receiving twice as much – possibly that's why I inflicted it, to punish this bad man of my split personality so that the good man could destroy the bad and remind him of the terrible things he's done.

So off I'd go in search of my other self in a bottle – wow was I sick.

8 Women

After I left I lived with my brother and his wife. On the surface I handled it quite well slotting into the old Johnny again but people did not see my pain. This was another vessel 'stretched' in the brain.

After some time there was a divorcee down the street who looked a cracker. I asked her out and within a few days my feet are under the table. We went to Minorca for a couple of months but over the whole period of time I wasn't really fair to her. If my second wife hadn't broken me I'm sure this relationship would have lasted longer and I would have been more loyal and faithful to her. We had a lot of fun but I wasted that relationship just like all the others.

How come when I was chatting anyone up in my head I was scoring the winning goal for my team or having a Guinness in the pub. Was it just because I thought I had to keep up the macho image or was I using women because of a dislike generally caused by my Mother's deception? It always had to be my decision to end a relationship, paying women back for what a woman had done to my dad.

I don't know if that is the reason for my cruelty or the real reason was that I was an out and out nutter – a chauvinist, egotist, big head or whatever name there is for such a person.

When this relationship ended I went to live in London and me and some mates went on a bender at lunchtime. At closing time we decided to get plenty of six packs and have a 'picnic' in Hyde Park. A Hot Dog vendor appeared and we ordered some food but got charged a lot and we thought this was because we sounded Northern which would label us as 'Divis'. I'm explosive and tip his cart upside down! There was a bunch of Japanese tourists taking pictures of everything. I think what got my temper to such a point was that after I refused to pay he offered me a lower price but my mates had already paid and so had the tourists.

There they were helping him to pick everything up, I often wonder if they thought it was the British custom of 'tipping' and did the same to another hot dog salesman further down the park!

9 The Holocaust

Almost there now, clock ticking away in my head. I was on a downer, mean and nasty drinking to ease my pain. With continuous drinking you can reach the peak of happiness then the guilt takes over and with more booze melancholy then the big one – HATE – a terrible condition to find yourself in. I had no outlet for my hate except anger – a real life Jeckyll and Hyde until finally November 18th 1978 the explosion in my brain, my personal holocaust.

I was drunk and fighting in the street, adrenalin flowing, blood pumping so quickly I suffered a near-fatal brain haemorrhage and was virtually given up for dead. Two brain operations and a stroke later I found myself in hospital.

Opening my eyes for the first time on regaining consciousness I looked at silhouettes in the room trying desperately to remember their significance, ladies in starched, crisp uniforms moving quickly from bed to bed folding back the sheets, tidying and feeding. I could remember them, they were nurses and something to do with hospitals.

I couldn't move my head sideways or lift it up because it felt heavy and anchored to the pillow. The nurses kept passing by like busying bees on a foxglove – so I was in hospital but what for, what had happened?

I couldn't remember.

The pressure increasing on my brain would only allow me to squint through blurred, lazy eyes and with chaotic double vision every nurse, doctor, auxiliary, cleaner and visitor were two – the hospital was overcrowded with people!

After I blinked a tightened nose blink the room would be halved of people again making me more confused and with a total loss of memory seconds after anything was said or done I was trapped in a time lapse of many different stages of my life.

If only I could remember what had happened. I suppose I'd been told many times yet it was instantly forgotten.

Whenever I 'spoke' I couldn't understand why people would turn away and ask others in the room 'What's he saying?' My mumbled screeching voice never seemed to have any impediment to me and I would wonder why all my visitors had suddenly gone deaf.

My short-term memory was non-existent. Mixed and jumbled memories of my life would reappear though never in any chronological order. One day I was ten then nineteen or thirty two. I would try desperately to put the pieces together but I was hopeless. My brain was permanently damaged.

10 Derby Royal Infirmary

My survival is a procession of stages but the most important is all due to a little girl in Derby Royal who had had a brain tumour operation. I lay in my bed day after day never walking to the day room and would move only to get out of bed whilst they made it and then climb quickly back in or sit in my 'high chair' with my 'turban' on looking very ill and pathetic. I was completely shocked and more importantly giving up on life.

This little girl of six or seven years of age would come to my bedside talking and talking and pestering me to come for walks. My family, doctors and nurses could never get me to exercise but this little girl did. She would take me all over the hospital wards. My memory was so bad that on being told something I'd quickly forget it and Julie would sound just like a little old lady when telling the nurses 'I've just shown him once and he's lost again!'

When the nurses saw us they all stopped what they were doing and shouted to each other 'Come and see this' or 'Look who's out of his bed.'

Well little Julie got me out of bed, she taught me my first steps again and gave me the will to carry on. We would walk hand in hand and formed a really touching relationship.

A few weeks after a moving farewell to her on my discharge I discovered little Julie had died and I broke my heart. God bless Julie xx

The Consultant and his team of doctors saved my life, their delicate surgery gave me breath again then Julie took over and gave me the will to go on. My brother and his wife had their turn with their love and the rest was up to me.

S'funny how the human being can laugh under the most traumatic circumstances like when I first learned to walk again bouncing round like Andy Pandy but you can still laugh!

In Derby hospital next to my bed was a chap called Jack, an ex-miner who had worked with my dad at one time. Poor chap had been in a car accident and there he was with broken limbs – arms, legs, back – (I top the story up a bit by saying he had only his eyes visible bandaged like a mummy) with legs in traction and worst of all he'd had brain surgery. He was in a bad way but when his wife told my family about it she said he was lucky though 'He was in the firm's car!'

One day I was having a smoke in the visitors' room when this little bloke stood up and snorted 'If you're going to smoke I'm going'

So Wrighty subtle as ever shouts "Well clear off then!"

The nurse came dashing over to me because I must not raise my blood pressure.

'What's the matter John? 'It's that bastard' pointing to the bloke 'on about us smoking.'

' You mean the Vicar. Has the Vicar upset you?'

I smiled about that when she went and gave ole Vic a right telling off!

When I was in hospital I used to remember different periods of my life, I could remember myself but never at a fixed age. After the brain operations I was thirty three years old but I was remembering times from years before. I would have a quick memory flash but then whatever age I was in the memory I stayed that age for the whole day.

On one such day my Uncle came to visit and told me he'd got married. I could remember his wife because I used to play with her daughter when we were young so in my mind I would go back to those times when I was ten then I would fall asleep still playing with the little girl. Then my ex-wife would visit but how could I have been married to her I'm only ten years old! The chaos got worse because on another visit my second wife came after the first – bigamy and I'm only ten.

These moments of being awake again caused more chaos – ex-girlfriends and ex-live in girlfriends would appear and although the gaps in real time stretched over many years to me it was now and I imagined a stream of women by my bedside demanding maintenance payments.

I was in a complete state of delirium. I would catch a glimpse of TV then go back to sleep again. During a visit from my brother and his wife I was convinced I was in a Prisoner of War hospital because I'd caught sight of Colditz on the TV.

'Psst, come here.'

'What John?'

'I'm over the wall tonight.'

'You're what?"

'I'm over the wall tonight.'

'Are you?

'Yeah, keep it quiet.'

Then I heard echoes of footsteps down the ward and a uniformed man appeared.

It was only an AA man wearing boots and a peaked cap visiting another patient!

I genuinely thought this holocaust would be over in a few months, like a plaster cast one day removed, stamp your foot and be healed.

I was never really aware of the severity of it all. S'pose that's how I've got this far, I really think I should have been called Johnny Wrong!

11 A Dedication

Because of the confusion and amnesia my belated thanks appear for Steve my brother and Bev. I couldn't ever have begun my book without them. I had always felt so strongly of how Bev and Steve had played a role, a leading role, in the early days but I never mentioned it – now I do.

At Derby they came every other night but the visiting is not where I give them credit. Back home we all had to learn to 'cope' with the dilemmas. They were my guardians literally feeding me, Steve bathing me both dressing me. I cannot describe on paper just how important a role they played. It would seem so trivial to mention the fact that the pair of them would cut my meat, wash my hair and fasten buttons (I couldn't cope with buttons).

I would like to dedicate this book to them in appreciation of their love and delicate care in those dark, dark days. Later my own home gave me a new identity but Bev and Steve gave me love. I came home from hospital so very confused and a memory that disappeared as fast as clicking your fingers but this love I received from them both was so very important to me. If I had gone anywhere else I don't think I would have come through 'cos besides washing and feeding me the one ingredient I needed to see and feel was love and they provided me with more than enough. I was very weak and very sensitive mentally as well as physically and they gave me strength when I really needed it.

ME WITH STEVE, BEV & FRIEND JIMMY

A lot of people thought they had done 'their bit' by visiting me in Derby and then that's it over, he's home so he's better. They had no idea what was to follow. I would hate to go through that mental pain again but Steve and Bev, 'this one's for you'. From a complete physical and mental wreck to what I'm becoming I want you to know I'm climbing back, I'm just over half way, when I get to the top I'll reach for you and give you a peg up. 'Gracias para todo.'

12 Going Home

When the nurse told me I could leave Derby Hospital my brain and memory could only remember how I used to look. Probably I thought I was more handsome than I really was 'cos memories are like that aren't they? I had this memory video of my life, of most things before November 1978 and I knew how I used to look good or bad whatever your taste but I could remember me. Then the biggest, worst, dramatic, horrific shock I'll ever have!

I really thought that under my 'turban' the Johnny I last remembered would appear just like the transformation from monster to doctor in Jeckyll and Hyde. I imagined as the bandage was lifted piece by piece my weight, hair even my colouring would appear as I remembered but then I was about to face my first shock.

I tried to put my clothes on. My jeans had more 'slack' than a colliery pithead! My shirt and sweater were literally hanging off me and even my shoes were slipping off – how can your feet lose weight? I walked by hanging onto Bev's shoulder. I should have learned from the very first shock that my whole life would be completely transformed. It was so frightening.

Now, seven years later, I still cannot quite believe the situation. It has been such a long time, everything seems alien to me. Simple things I could do before my operation I know are gone and will never come back. I'll never be like I was . . .

I used to hate old people before my operations and didn't have any time for them at all but while staying with Steve and Bev I formed a really touching, loving relationship with Bertha, the seventy nine year old lady next door. I used to walk like 'Bill and Ben the Flowerpot Men' with hardly any balance at all. She was losing her balance and the use of her legs through age and because of this she had to push a pushchair to go shopping.

One day I asked if I could go with her and help her as much as I could with me leaning on her pushchair having to tell Bertha at seventy nine not to walk so fast please!

Well over the months and later years my condition improved and Bertha's deteriorated with age. She eventually became housebound moving from room to room to room on a frame so I would shop for her and on a Friday we would have fish and chips.

She was also indirectly and unwittingly very helpful to me in perfecting my speech. Speech therapy was most important of all in my relearning process. As the years went by Bertha became my speech therapist simply by not wearing her hearing aid.

My brain still heard a good voice whenever I spoke but people still couldn't understand so with Bertha saying 'What?' every time I spoke and me having to shout (shouting carefully with a speech impediment is very difficult) my speech gradually improved.

My socialist feelings really ignited when listening to the old lady talk of her mother and father's struggles – Dickensian times in the 20th Century – she would weep for them and their struggle. It really does disgust me when there is so much wealth yet at the other end of the scale so much poverty. Why should the system of life be like this?

Bertha became many things to me and as well as my speech therapist she helped my memory. Because of her age her memory was fading so I would have to concentrate and be ready for her half way through a sentence asking 'What was I on about John?'

When I could prompt her I would be so pleased with myself.

She finished her life in an old people's home and I used to go and push her in a wheelchair through the streets. I do not write about this relationship without getting sadly happy thinking of poor old Bertha and this is not an old cliché 'cos they really did throw away the mould when they made Bert!

My brother and his wife had been very patient but I felt ready to move on. I wanted to take the pressure off them and be more independent in a place of my own. Some days I was excited with what I had achieved then others I became too pessimistic in thinking that recovery would never be complete.

This was the longest hangover in history!

13 New Freedom

'There's a freedom you find on your own that's nearly worth what you pay'
– Kris Kristofferson.

Troglodyte Person

As soon as I was able to 'cope' on my own I moved to a council bungalow a few miles out of Leicester. I became a recluse for three years. I stopped swearing, became celibate, didn't drink or smoke and became a Jehovah's Witness. I also grew my hair, beard and fingernails writing at the time:

May 5

'In my new home with all this simplicity I have become a Troglodyte person. Yeah, that's a new one for you eh? Well it's a type of recluse, a cave dweller. I am discovering new words then writing them down to eventually memorise them. I have a dictionary so it's a form of learning. When this is all over a lot of my knowledge will be self-taught. I'm re-educating myself.'

May 13

'I wonder if my courage will remain with me to complete my goal or will I fade and shrink? I do not want to quit and every day try my hardest to fight back but sometimes the mental pain is very strong. I'm growing my beard again, it must be some sort of mental camouflage. I feel terribly naked when I'm clean shaven. I've had three or four bushy beards and each time I've shaved them off I feel bare, recognisable, vulnerable so I grow them again. Stupid really but it does give me some comfort having one so I must keep it on. Sometimes in my condition it's nice to hide.'

May 14

'Since I've been here in my solitude my 'new' brain has been allowed to settle without any influence whatsoever so whoever or whatever kind of person I've become this time it's down to me. My isolation has been very therapeutic and another lesson from my illness.'

May 20

'My new character is not complete and will not be so until I recover totally. It will keep changing slightly and hopefully definite traits will remain with me for life. I have become a recluse, a man who's 'into' celibacy. I don't have any sexual fantasies, hang ups or whatever. I have not become gay – there are no thoughts of sex at all. I have become honest, honest to myself. At this time of my life it is important for me to be honest with myself and women play no tunes for me. This vow of celibacy is for no religious reasons simply for myself.'

I was so close to insanity at this time and often contemplated suicide. I wrote a note about who should have what and even planned my own funeral and who was to be invited.

June 2

'Still the decay continues. I've reached the age of thirty seven and I don't think I can go much further. If only I could come to terms with the advantages I have instead of always thinking of the disadvantages. What others see is an improvement to them but to me I see a totally different image if only they could identify with it all.

It will not leave me, my skull is so heavy, not like "This is heavy man" but I'm 'top heavy'. I remember a line in a song before all this happened – "Wake me up, this ain't me" and that's how I feel now waiting for a miracle.

Some days I was more optimistic than others. Music helped me a lot and Kris Kristofferson's lyric "There's a freedom you find on your own that's nearly worth what you pay" seemed so very true.

Don't just read the words think about them. I'm on my own now and I've discovered a new kind of freedom and it's worth what I've paid.

July 11

'Life is such a change for me now. I find it very difficult to venture outside my front door and I love being on my own writing, playing music, peace. I still have difficulty walking so I guess that's a big influence on why I stay indoors for such long periods but t be perfectly honest I do love being on my own - like when I'm writing this book I love the isolation. I can only do a short period at a time because my brain tires very quickly but it's stimulating and I enjoy it. I am very proud of my book, I really am. It has nearly all my feelings down at the time of writing and when I have long rest periods from it and then continue I can see my feelings in writing. For me, it's all here. Some words describe just how I was feeling at the time and even things I've erased tell me something.'

'From my lounge window I've just seen an old lady who is blind feeling her way down the street with a stick. It's incredible that people continue to fight back against such terrible ordeals. It's possible that I might recover completely but if not I can still see. I must keep reminding myself that even in my condition now I am very fortunate. I don't think twice about looking out of the window and that lady just keeps tapping away.

It's difficult because you can't really identify with the problem but if you just try and close your eyes for a minute it must be horrific.

I don't get a smug feeling at someone less fortunate than me, I do get a sense of relief.'

14 Headway

Eventually with family support I joined a group called 'Headway' which offered support to brain injured people and their families.

We all sat in a big circle, social workers, patients, psychologists and families. We discussed what problems we had faced, what we hoped for in the future and how we could become a group to help people who are thrown into this pit of confusion to fend for themselves. I certainly would have found it helpful to talk to someone who had suffered something as drastic as my illness at the beginning of my recovery - someone to say 'hey, hang on there. I was like you some time back so have faith, one day at a time.'

At our very first meeting I went in my best suit, short hair, beard shaved off and looked a 'bit flash' I suppose and even fellow patients were fooled by my appearance. You see my condition is not visible now apart from a slight slur in my speech and a walking stick. People tend to go by visible appearance and that is a totally wrong attitude to take with something a serious as a brain injury but it proved to me in this crazy system that the first judgement is with the eye. We must not judge this way, brain injury is a hidden disability.

Some months later the Headway group asked me to make a speech at a cheese and wine party to give encouragement to others who have suffered like me. I was very nervous but felt it was something I had to do so, dressed as smartly as I could took a deep breath and began . . .

First of all my sincere thanks for the help and concern from the professional people of our group and also the relatives because without you there simply would be no group. We, the patients, with our insight into the despair of brain injury, can possibly speak of our ideas of what we would like to organise but we really need your help and understanding. From my own point of view I have found our meetings very refreshing, stimulating and encouraging.

It is nice to be accepted as a man fighting to regain his health and not as some 'prize dumbo!' Each individual who suffers a brain injury has a different recovery. For me it's made me aware that my life before my haemorrhage was a complete waste. If I don't recover completely I have the consolation that I am a much better person than ever before. I don't want to bore anyone with the sordid description of my life but I feel I must clarify how much I've changed. I want to reveal it. I want to help.'

I went on to tell them about my Dad's suicide and how I was then told, at his funeral, that he was not my real Dad. How this had led to anger, depression, drinking and violence and the torment of having two personalities who were at war with each other constantly.

'Coming to terms with my illness has not been easy. In the early days I genuinely thought my life was over and I cannot describe the torment of my first year back in civilisation but gradually a new person was emerging. Things I thought were boring in my previous life were gradually becoming part of me giving me a new foundation to rebuild my life. What and who I am today is how I want to be judged. I have ambition now'.

I told them about loving Spain and how I could speak some Spanish before my brain injury and how going back there was a driving force in my efforts to regain my health. I would also like to study and re-educate myself on many subjects.

'The whole purpose of me becoming a member of Headway is to reach out to the people when they first suffer the shock and ordeal of major brain surgery and help them overcome those traumatic days – the beginning should be our aim.

I've only scratched the surface but perhaps fellow sufferers can identify with me.

Some patients might go back to their old way of life but me, I never go backwards only forwards. I've been there and I don't want to go back.'

I then told them about writing this book – *'It's no Steinbeck or*

Hemingway but I'm very proud of it so get your orders in now!'

I sat down at the end of the most important speech I've ever made and received a standing ovation. It was a very emotional moment and a real milestone in my rehabilitation.

HEADWAY SPEECH

15 From Therapy to a Dream

I have had many hours, days, months and now years to reflect on my life before and after my haemorrhage. I'm now letting a bit of aggression back only this time I'll try to channel it to different quarters. I've been 'dead and buried' by many people and by others branded as some kind of nutter, a vegetable but I'm fulfilling my purpose in life to get some kind of achievement and that will be my two fingers in the air to all the pathetic people who are so black and white and negative in their outlook on life.

For the last couple of weeks I've been going out everywhere without my walking stick. That's another barrier I've broken through. My walking is not very steady but it's a truly great feeling to walk with my hands in my pockets on a casual stroll. These are things I must keep telling myself – one ambition fulfilled and such a good feeling. I must keep spotting these small signs and take encouragement from them. With my walking stick practically unemployed it would be quite easy to forget that part of my illness but I don't think so. I shall never be complacent again.

Over the years my story has grown and I have grown with it. All the hate has disappeared over the pages, perhaps only I can see that but each paragraph is just how I was thinking, how the jigsaw in my brain was slotting into place.

There have been times when I didn't write for months to give myself time to reflect on life and it was during one of these 'rest periods' that I found myself at a party and to cut a long story short I met a woman who followed me home and my vow of celibacy was broken! Suddenly I was alive again and my journey back into the real world had begun.

I wrote this book to help judge my progress and I think it has done just that. Yeah, the writing could be better but it's the thinking that's been the success.

As I finish the final chapter I hope I have captured some of the heartbreak and physical and mental pain I suffered. My friends and family could not cope with the strange person I had become – I was not the Johnny they knew.

It was hard for them to accept but if I had doubts about my new character I would have packed it in by now. I have no self doubts. I know when I recover completely I will have enough determination to fulfil my ambitions.

I miss my Dad more now I think than before my haemorrhage, it would have been nice to have chats with him but I like to think he knows I'm coming good. I've served my apprenticeship in the misery trade – suicide, broken marriages and now a haemorrhage. I've been there and I'll try very hard not to go there again.

There was a time when I couldn't hold a pen – now I've written a book – not bad eh?

S'funny how you never laugh at the time though, innit?

John Wright

POSTSCRIPT

This book was discarded, unfinished before being first published in 1988 ten years after John's haemorrhage. At the time he was living independently and working for Leicester City Council's 'Meals on Wheels' service.

In 1998 he met Lindsay Louise and three years later in November 2001 they married and had many very happy years together until sadly in 2011 Lindsay died on September 22 having lost her very courageous fight against cancer.

John still has problems with short-term memory. He has had several further operations and experiences physical pressure on his brain which impacts significantly on his life.

Now in 2013 he is trying to rebuild his life as a single man and getting his book republished has given him a new interest.

'Happiness is sadness with a smile'

NOVEMBER 17, 2001 -
MARRIAGE TO LINDSAY LOUISE

43

Lightning Source UK Ltd.
Milton Keynes UK
UKOW06f0320011217
313623UK00005B/104/P